# *Fallen Words*

A Collection of New and Original

Rakugo Stories

**KRISTINE OHKUBO**

Copyright © 2023 by Kristine Ohkubo.

All rights reserved. No part of this publication may be reproduced, distributed, or transmitted in any form or by any means, including photocopying, recording, or other electronic or mechanical methods, without the prior written permission of the author, except in the case of brief quotations embodied in critical reviews and certain other noncommercial uses permitted by copyright law. For permission requests, contact the author using the webpage address provided below.

https://kristineohkubo.wixsite.com/nonfiction-author

Fallen Words: *A Collection of New and Original Rakugo Stories* /Kristine Ohkubo. —1st ed.

ISBN 978-1-0880-0077-9

# Table of Contents

Introduction ................................................................... 3

The Substitute Dog: An Overview ....................................... 8

    The Substitute Dog (*Okage-inu*) ................................... 14

The Lesser Known Tales of the Brothers Grimm ................ 27

    A Child's Coins (*Kodomo no okane*) ............................. 31

    I Want a Divorce (*Rikon shitai*) .................................... 43

    There's a Frog in My Rice Porridge (*Okayu ni kaeru ga iru*) ...... 49

Börte's Kidnapping: A True Story ....................................... 57

    Börte's Kidnapping (*Borute no yūkai*) ............................ 62

Mongolian Pronunciation Guide .......................................... 72

List of Illustrations ............................................................ 73

Works Cited ..................................................................... 74

About the Author .............................................................. 76

The Rakugo Collection ...................................................... 79

# Introduction

Fallen words is the literal English translation of the Japanese term *rakugo* (落語). What is rakugo? Noriko Watanabe, an assistant professor at Baruch College, once described rakugo as "a sitcom with one person playing all the parts."[1] In that regard the statement is quite true. Rakugo is a minimalistic performance art enacted by a lone storyteller who portrays all of the characters in the story while utilizing only two props, a *sensu* (a paper fan) and a *tenugui* (a hand towel), to help convey the narrative. The performer seamlessly switches from one character to another by changing their voice, facial expression, mannerisms, and accent to fit the individual who is speaking.

Since rakugo does not utilize elaborate sets and costumes, mannerisms are key to portraying specific characters in the story. For example, a subtle change in where and how the storyteller places their hands signals the change of character during the storytelling process. If the storyteller folds their hands daintily on their lap, the audience understands that they are portraying a female character. Sometimes the performer will touch the collar of their kimono and appear demure when portraying a female role. On the other hand, by extending their elbows outward and placing their hands on their hips the storyteller can portray a big, burly samurai.

Additionally, the two props are given a great deal of versatility in the stories as they are used to represent a wide range of items. For instance,

---

[1] "Rakugo." New World Encyclopedia, 2008, https://www.newworldencyclopedia.org/entry/Rakugo#cite_note-3.

a sensu can represent a writing brush, a pair of chopsticks, or a pipe. A tenugui can represent a wallet, a *tabako-ire* (Edo era tobacco pouch), or a book.[2]

*Rakugoka* (storytellers) also utilize the rule of *kami-shimo* or stage left and stage right when they are relating their stories. This rule is related to Japan's vertical society and social ranking system. When the performer is portraying a character who is older or holds a higher status in society such as a father or a samurai, they usually face the *shimote* or stage right side when speaking. When the storyteller is portraying a person who is younger or holds a lower status such as a female or a child character, they usually speak their lines facing the *kamite* or stage left side of the stage from the performer's perspective. [3]

The popular narrative art of rakugo dates back to the Edo period (1603–1867) and consists of a repertoire of more than 500 classical stories. These stories were seldom written down and have been passed down as an oral tradition from master to disciple over the centuries. However, there were some early performers such as Sanyutei Encho (April 1, 1839 – August 11, 1900), who actually had their stories published.

Encho cooperated with Takusari Koki, the inventor of *sokki* or the Japanese shorthand system. While Encho recited his tales on stage, students from Takusari's stenography school sat backstage and used the new system of shorthand to transcribe his stories, which were later made

---

[2] Ohkubo, Kristine. Talking About Rakugo 1: The Japanese Art of Storytelling. 2nd ed., 2022, p. 6.
[3] Kanariya, Eiraku. "Basic Rules for Performing Rakugo." Eiraku's 100 English Rakugo Scripts (Volume 1), vol. 1, 2022, p. 14.

i. Sanyutei Encho

into a shorthand book and serialized in newspapers. Some of his stories were even remade as kabuki plays.[4]

In addition to the *koten* (classical) rakugo stories, there is a substantial collection of *shinsaku* (new and original) rakugo stories written and performed by contemporary rakugoka on a continuing basis. While these modern stories are usually inspired by warmhearted daily life drama or current events, they still generally incorporate characters that have been used since the Edo period.[5]

Although the majority of rakugo tales are comical in nature, there are stories whose central theme incorporates human interest or macabre topics.

Before getting into the main story, a rakugoka warms up with a *makura* or a short funny tale that is related to the performance. The makura is a multi-purpose tool in the storyteller's arsenal. It can be used to amuse the audience and get them to relax before the start of the main story, to lead the audience into the main topic of the story using a related scene, or as a means to set up the final punchline.[6]

---

[4] Ohkubo, Kristine. Talking About Rakugo 1, pp. 25-26.
[5] Ackerman, Stefanie. "Rakugo: The Traditional Japanese Art of Storytelling." Japan Wonder Travel Blog, Japan Wonder Travel Blog, 7 Sept. 2022, https://blog.japanwondertravel.com/rakugo-japanese-storytelling-36260#:~:text=Modern%20rakugo%20material%20is%20usually,simply%20reproducing%20classic%20rakugo%20sketches.
[6] Yu, A. C. "Rakugo (Japanese Traditional Comic Storytelling, or the Comic Story Itself) - Japanese Wiki Corpus." Rakugo (Japanese Traditional Comic Storytelling, or the Comic Story Itself) - Japanese Wiki Corpus, https://www.japanese-wiki-corpus.org/culture/Rakugo%20(Japanese%20Traditional%20Comic%20Storytelling,%20or%20the%20Comic%20Story%20Itself).html.

The story typically ends with a punchline known as an *ochi* (fall). The ochi can be delivered in the form of a joke, a *dajare* (pun), by returning to the beginning of the story, or by turning things or positions around (*sakasa*), among other things.[7] Current Kamigata rakugo storyteller, Katsura Bunshi, is among the most prolific in the world of rakugo. To date, he has produced 300 original rakugo stories.[8]

The wonderful thing about rakugo is that each rakugo performer conveys the story to their audience in their own unique way. Performers often change the original story to better suit their audience; taking into account the time and place of the performance. As a result, not only will an audience be able to enjoy different renditions of the same story delivered by different storytellers, but they can also witness the same storyteller slightly altering the story to match the milieu. In this sense, rakugo never gets old.

As the author/ editor of three rakugo books introducing English-speaking audiences to Japan's delightful storytelling tradition, I thought it would be fun to compile and release a collection of my own original English rakugo stories. I hope these stories will enlighten and entertain you.

---

[7] Yu, A. C. "Ochi (the Punch Line of a Joke) - Japanese Wiki Corpus." Ochi (the Punch Line of a Joke) - Japanese Wiki Corpus, https://www.japanese-wiki-corpus.org/culture/Ochi%20(the%20punch%20line%20of%20a%20joke).html.
[8] "桂文枝 (6代目)." Wikipedia, Wikimedia Foundation, 30 Nov. 2022, 桂文枝 (6代目) - Wikipedia.

# *The Substitute Dog: An Overview*

Japan's *Edo jidai* (Edo period) lasted for 264 years and was characterized by unprecedented economic growth, a strict social hierarchy, isolationist foreign policies, a stable population, peace, and the popular enjoyment of arts and culture.

By the mid-18th century, Edo's (modern Tokyo) population had grown to over one million, likely making it the most populous city in the world at the time. But what accounted for this stable population despite the low birth rates and recurring famines?

For one thing, beginning in 1635, Tokugawa Iemitsu, the third shogun of the Tokugawa dynasty, required all the *daimyo* (the domanial lords) to maintain households in the administrative capital of Edo and reside there for several months every other year. For another, the Tokugawa government enforced strict travel regulations on all of its citizens regardless of their social status.

The *Sakoku* (literally "chained country") isolationist policy of the Edo period severely limited interactions and trade between Japan and other countries. The policy banned nearly all foreign nationals from entering Japan while preventing common Japanese people from leaving the country. Failure to adhere to the policy was punishable by death.

The Tokugawa shogunate also controlled and limited every aspect of national travel to an extent unparalleled in the pre-industrial world.

Ordinary Japanese citizens were required to obtain a permit to travel in and out of Edo.

Travel was confined to five roads known as the *Gokaido*, the busiest of which was the *Tokaido* (literally East Sea road). Running along the southern coast of Japan's main island, the Tokaido extended from Edo to Kyoto.

The shogunate designated post towns along these roads. They also set up official inns at some of the towns to house the samurai traveling on official business, as well as the daimyo traveling between their domains and Edo. The system was set up for official use, but other travelers were permitted to use the well-maintained roads without fear of being accosted by bandits. In fact, ordinary people traveled more frequently and easily along the roads of Tokugawa Japan than possibly any place on the globe.

These roads, however, were controlled through a system of fifty-three checkpoint barriers known as the *sekisho*, at which travelers had to show a permit to pass. The sekisho were implemented during the early part of the Edo period and were part of the shogunate's framework to enforce peace at a time when the Warring States period (1467-1615) was just ending.

The sekisho were spread out strategically to check for movements of troops and guns, as well as to stop the daimyo from removing their wives and children from Edo, where they were kept as hostages of the shogunate. The sekisho were surrounded by palisades and placed in areas that were difficult to pass. The checkpoints were surrounded by a network of villages tasked with watching the area for those attempting to circumvent the system.

The sekisho system employed by both the shogunate and the domains kept an eye out for wanted criminals and samurai fleeing their domains. The system also kept peasants on their land and stopped samurai from traveling anywhere except on official business. The sekisho discouraged women from traveling by utilizing a far more complicated application process for women's permits than for men's permits. Many sekisho did not even allow women to pass, instead funneling all female travelers through the few sekisho that would stringently inspect the women to check if they matched the descriptions on the permits they were carrying. For instance, a sekisho would deny a woman passage if her hair was judged to be cut and her permit said it was uncut. This ensured that the women would stay at home when the men had to travel on business, guaranteeing that families would not leave a domain for greener pastures.

Following the need for business travel, the next most common reason for travel during the Edo period was religious pilgrimage. As a matter of fact, Edo period literature is full of satire about pilgrims whose only religious practice was buying a handful of amulets at the shrine to prove they had been there. Most pilgrims were probably serious in their devotion, but their visit to the shrine was usually a part of an enjoyable vacation. Among those who could afford it, vacations lasting several months, leisurely wandering around Japan from one famous sight to another, were quite common.

But the growing popularity of travel during the Edo period was mostly tied to prosperity. To travel, a farmer or merchant needed both money and the ability to leave home with their farm or business carrying on without interruption. So what happened if people could not obtain a permit, or could not afford to go on a religious pilgrimage? The practice of using an *okage-inu* (おかげ犬) became popular during the Edo period. An okage-inu was a dog that would visit the shrine on behalf of the individual.

During the Edo period it was common for people to visit the Ise Grand Shrine, the most revered Shinto shrine in Japan. This once in a lifetime pilgrimage was known as *okage-mairi*. People of all classes would partake in this pilgrimage; however, some people were unable to make the trip for various reasons and sent an animal on their behalf instead.

For many, white dogs were the animal of choice, as it was a common belief that they possessed a certain spiritual quality that made them the perfect choice for visiting the shrine. The dogs sent to the Ise Grand Shrine were often identified by the *shimenawa* straw ropes hung around their necks. They also carried bags containing money that was to be given to the shrine priest and go toward the care of the dogs during their journey. The roundtrip journey from Edo to Ise could take over one month, and the dogs relied on the kindness of strangers along the way.

There are stories of dogs traveling from all over Japan to the Ise Grand Shrine, receiving food and lodging, traveling with impromptu companions, and ultimately arriving back home with an amulet from the shrine.

*ii. Asakichi Inn dating back to the Edo period (Furuichi)*

*iii. The Substitute Dog (Okage-inu)*

# The Substitute Dog (*Okage-inu*)

*Characters:*

| | |
|---|---|
| **I:** | Inkyo |
| **H:** | Hachigoro |
| **HAN:** | Hanji |

---

*With the creation of the Tokugawa shogunate in 1603, Japan finally said good-bye to the near-constant civil war and social upheaval that existed during the Sengoku era or the Warring States period.*

*The Edo period, which followed lasted for 264 years and brought with it peace, economic growth, and the popular enjoyment of arts and culture.*

*During this period, the shogunate constructed well-maintained roads on which ordinary citizens could travel without fear of being accosted by bandits. In fact, ordinary people traveled more frequently and easily in Tokugawa Japan than possibly any place on the globe.*

| | |
|---|---|
| **H:** | Hey, Hanji! |
| | Where have you been? |
| **HAN:** | Hey, Hachi! You crazy bastard. |
| | Did you miss me? |
| **H:** | You're my best friend, of course I did. |
| | Where did you go, huh? |
| | You were gone for over a month! |
| | Why were you gone for such a long time? |

**HAN:** Well, I went on a pilgrimage.

**H:** A pil….?

How do you ride a pil…whatever you said?

**HAN:** It's not something you ride on.

It's a journey to a shrine.

It can lead to personal transformation.

Aaaah! Hachi I am a changed man!

**H:** So, you're not Hanji any longer?

**HAN:** What do you mean?

**H:** You just said you're a changed man.

So who are you?

**HAN:** No, no, you got it all wrong!

By transformation, I meant spiritual awakening.

**H:** So you were asleep all this time?

**HAN:** Of course not!

**H:** So where did you go?

**HAN:** I went to the Ise Grand Shrine.

**H:** Where is that?

**HAN:** It's in Mie, of course.

Everyone knows that!

Even you must've heard of it.

Millions of people visit that shrine on a pilgrimage.

**H:** I thought you said you couldn't ride a partridge.

**HAN:** PILGRIMAGE!

Traveling to a shrine is described as being on a pilgrimage.

|   |   |
|---|---|
|   | Where did you get that hair-brained idea about riding a partridge? |
| **H:** | You said it. |
| **HAN:** | I did not! |
|   | Anyway, it was great fun. |
| **H:** | Fun? What's so fun about spending time with a bunch of priests? |
| **HAN:** | Well, the pilgrimage road passes through the entertainment district of Furuichi. |
|   | Furuichi has lots of inns, playhouses, and… girls… (*wink!*) |
| **H:** | Girls? |
| **HAN:** | You know…girls…(*wink!*) |
| **H:** | Oh? Oh, those girls! Hahahahahaha. |
|   | (*Slaps Hanji on the shoulder*) |
|   | You must've had a really good time on your pillage. |
| **HAN:** | Who said anything about pillaging Furuichi! |
| **H:** | You did! |
| **HAN:** | I did not! |
|   | I went on a pilgrimage to the Ise Shrine! |
|   | I ate wonderful food, toured amazing sites, watched several plays… |
| **H:** | (*Interrupts*) So when did you have time to visit the shrine? |
| **HAN:** | (*Clears his throat*) |
|   | Eh…err….I visited the shrine first and later did all those things. See this? It's an amulet that I bought at the shrine. This proves that I was there! |

| | |
|---|---|
| **H:** | (*Takes the amulet and examines it*) |
| | What's to say you didn't spend ALL of your time in Furuichi playing around with the girls (*wink*!) and you just bought this amulet to say you visited the shrine? |
| **HAN:** | WHAT?!? Give me that! |
| | (*Rips the amulet out of Hachi's hands*) |
| **H:** | Well? |
| **HAN:** | So long Hachi! |
| | You bastard! |
| **H:** | Why did he get so angry all of a sudden? |
| | If I were him, I would have spent all my time playing around. |
| | Who wants to go on a trip and spend all their time with a bunch of priests anyway? |
| | Maybe I'll go to Furuichi! |
| | Hahahahaha….sounds like a lot of fun. I can eat wonderful food, tour amazing sites, and watch several plays. |
| | Ah! Who wants to do that? I want to play with the girls…(*wink*!) |

*Never having traveled outside of Edo (modern day Tokyo), Hachi had no idea how to go about it. He visited his old friend Inkyo who lived down the alley to ask for his advice.*

| | |
|---|---|
| **H:** | *Knock, knock, knock!* |
| | Hey Inkyo-san! Are you home? |

*Knock, knock, knock!*

Inkyo-san!

**I:** I'm coming….I'm coming…hold your horses.

(*Opens the door*)

Oh! Hachi, it's you!

Come in, come in.

**H:** Inkyo-san, have you ever gone on a pil…pil….

**I:** Yes, I take several pills each day.

You know at my age you can't live without pills.

**H:** No, no, I mean, have you ever visited a shrine?

**I:** Of course I have.

At my age you visit shrines quite often.

The older you get the more religious you become.

**H:** Have you ever visited the Ise Grand Shrine?

**I:** Of course, who hasn't?

**H:** (*Looks down seemingly forlorn*)

Well… I haven't. I'd like to go, just once.

I'd like to go on a pawnage!

**I:** (*Glances at Hachi with one eye open and his hand under his chin*)

Well (*pause*)…

You may need to sell a few things to raise the money for the trip Hachi…

**H:** (*Interrupts Inkyo*)

I don't have anything to sell.

**I:** I see.

Well, going on a pilgrimage to the Ise Shrine is the best way to travel these days.

You know, because the shrine is a sanctuary, there are no security checkpoints along the way. You can travel freely without a permit from the government.

Plus, the two main shrines of Ise are joined by a road that passes through (*hee-hee-hee*) the entertainment district of Furuichi. (*wink!*)

**H:** Hey! That's exactly what Hanji said.

Furuichi has lots of girls. (*wink!*)

**I:** (*With a wide grin and a dreamy look in his old eyes*)

It certainly does!

**H:** What? Inkyo-san, you know about the girls? (*wink!*)

**I:** Ehem…(*clears his throat*)

Of course I do! I was young once. (*hee-hee-hee*)

**H:** So, how do I go on a stowage? Huh?

Inkyo-san, tell me.

**I:** No, no, you won't need to take a boat to get there.

It isn't too difficult really.

All you need is time and money. Time and money.

**H:** Well, I don't have anything to do, so I have all the time in the world.

As for money…I'm a little short on that. (*Let's out an embarrassed laugh*)

I borrowed some money from Kuma yesterday to buy a bowl of soba noodles from the soba stand.

| | |
|---|---|
| **I:** | You borrowed money from me the week before to buy some sake! |
| **H:** | I did? Oh, yes, I did. Hahaha…(*Grins*) |
| | I must have forgotten. |
| **I:** | (*Glances at Hachi with one eye open*) Errr – well…. |
| | The Ise Grand Shrine is about 200 miles from Edo, and it can take you over a month to travel there and back. |
| | You will need money for the inns along the way and for food. |
| **H:** | How much money? |
| **I:** | More than what you have! |
| **H:** | I see. *(Looks downtrodden)* |
| | All I want is an amulet from the shrine to show off like Hanji did. |
| **I:** | Well, there is a way you can get an amulet. |
| **H:** | There is? (*Suddenly reinvigorated*) |
| **I:** | Yes. You can send your pet dog to the shrine in your place. |
| **H:** | (*Confused*) My pet dog? |
| **I:** | Yes! For various reasons some people can't go on a pilgrimage and they send their pet dogs to the shrine on their behalf. |
| | A pilgrimage to the shrine is called *okage-mairi,* and a dog who makes the journey on behalf of its master is called an *okage-inu*. |
| **H:** | Can a dog really travel to the shrine by itself? |

**I:** Well, people will help the dog.

There are many pilgrims on the road going to the Grand Ise Shrine.

They will see the dog and they will help it on its journey.

**H:** When I see a dog roaming the streets around here I yell at it and tell it to get the hell out.

How do people know the dog is going to the shrine?

**I:** The dogs have *shimenawa* straw ropes hung around their necks.

**H:** I see.

But even a dog will need food and a place to rest.

A month is a long time to be gone.

**I:** You are right Hachi.

The dogs are sent on their journey with bags of money, or a rope of coins tied around their necks. This money will go toward their care.

You will also need money to give to the shrine priest once the dog gets there.

**H:** Give money to the priest?

Those greedy priests!

I'd rather spend the money in Furuichi and play with the girls. (*wink!*)

**I:** Well, you want the dog to bring back an amulet for you don't you?

**H:** Hanji had an amulet, but I don't believe he went to the shrine.

Inkyo-san, I have a problem.

| | |
|---|---|
| **I:** | What's that? |
| **H:** | I don't have a pet dog. |
| **I:** | Maybe you can borrow a dog. |
| | White dogs are the most suited for visiting shrines. |
| **H:** | Yes! Maybe I could. |
| | Hey! Hanji has a dog! |
| | Thanks Inkyo-san! |
| | *Hachi departs for Hanji's house. Hanji is outside when he arrives.* |
| **H:** | Hey Hanji! |
| **HAN:** | Oh, it's you again. |
| | (*Growls at Hachi*) What do you want? |
| **H:** | Hey! Can't I visit my best friend? |
| **HAN:** | How can you call yourself my best friend after what you said to me? |
| **H:** | Was I wrong? |
| **HAN:** | Get the hell out Hachi! |
| **H:** | Hey Hanji, hold on. Do you still have that dog? |
| **HAN:** | Pochi? Yeah, I still have him. Why do you want to know? |
| **H:** | Can I borrow him? |
| **HAN:** | Why? |
| **H:** | Well, I want to send it to the shrine. |
| **HAN:** | What? |
| **H:** | Inkyo-san said that when people can't go to the shrine they send their pet dogs. |
| | Can I send Pochi Hanji? Can I? |
| **HAN:** | Well, I guess I can let you borrow him. |

**H:** GREAT!!!!

**HAN:** Do you have money?

**H:** You want me to pay you for letting me borrow your dog?

**HAN:** No!!! You need to have money for the dog's food and for the shrine priest.

Didn't Inkyo-san tell you that, you oaf?

**H:** Yeah, he did…but…

**HAN:** But what?

**H:** I don't have any money.

**HAN:** How can you expect to make the pilgrimage to the shrine if you don't have any money?

**H:** Can you let me borrow some money?

**HAN:** What? You want me to let you borrow my dog and you want me to give you money too? That's absurd!

**H:** Oh come on Hanji. You are my best friend. I would do it for you if you asked me to.

**HAN:** I wouldn't ask you!

**H:** Why not?

**HAN:** Because you don't have any money or a dog!

Besides, in all of the years I have known you, have I ever asked you for anything?

**H:** No…But didn't you say that visiting the shrine made you a changed man?

**HAN:** I did…

**H:** Come on Hanji, just this once.

Pleeeeeeease! I will never ask you for anything ever again.

**HAN:** Never again? Hmmmm…
OK. If it'll get you off my back, I'll do it.
I'll let you borrow my dog and I will give you money for its journey.

**H:** You are the best Hanji! You really are!
*Hachi leaves Hanji's place with Pochi and a small bag of money. Hachi is looking at the bag of money and talking to himself as he and Pochi approach his house where he intends to get the dog ready of its pilgrimage.*

**H:** Gee! That was sure nice of Hanji to let me borrow you and borrow this money.
(*The dog barks*)
I could have a really good time in Furuichi with this money!
(*The dog barks again*)
Who wants to waste money on some greedy priest anyway?
Amulet, shamulet…who needs it?
With this money I can play with the girls in Furuichi and drink lots of sake.
Woo-hoo-hoo! Wouldn't that be fun!
Don't you think so Pochi?
(*The dog barks in agreement*)
*In no time, the two arrive at Hachi's house. As Hachi prepares the dog for his journey, Pochi is very eager—wagging his tale and barking excitedly. Hachi tries to*

*calm the dog down. He cautions him to go directly to the shrine and not to take a detour to Furuichi.*

**H:** Hey! Calm down will you. What are you so excited about?

I've never seen a dog so eager to visit a shrine.

Calm down, calm down!

*Hachi opens the door and Pochi takes off running.*

*A month passes and he does not return.*

*Two months pass and he still has not come back.*

**H:** I wonder what happened to Pochi?

He should've been back by now.

I wonder if he went to Hanji's place instead?

I better go check on him.

*Arrives at Hanji's house.*

**H:** Hey Hanji!

**HAN:** Hachi! You're just the man I wanted to see!

**H:** I am?

**HAN:** Yes! Do you know what happened to my dog?

**H:** No, that's why I came to see you.

Has he not returned?

**HAN:** You know full well that he has not!

In fact, I heard from my neighbor who just returned from a pilgrimage to the shrine.

**H:** You did?

**HAN:** I did! And do you know what he told me?

**H:** No, what?

| | |
|---|---|
| **HAN:** | He said he spotted Pochi in Furuichi playing a lap dog to a cute girl! |
| **H:** | Whaaat? |
| **HAN:** | Yes! And when the neighbor tried to bring him back, he bit the neighbor. |
| **H:** | Huh? |
| **HAN:** | You've done it this time Hachi! (*Rolling up his sleeve*) You borrowed my dog; you borrowed my money, and now you are living on borrowed time!<br>(*Hachi takes off running*)<br>Hey, where do you think you're going? |
| **H:** | I'm going to substitute for Pochi in Furuichi! |

# The Lesser Known Tales of the Brothers Grimm

It has been over 200 years since Jacob and Wilhelm Grimm released their collection of children's stories titled *Children's and Household Tales* (German: *Kinder- und Hausmärchen*). First published on December 20, 1812, the collection contained 86 stories. By the time the seventh edition was published in 1857, the collection had grown to include 210 unique fairy tales.[9]

Despite their ultimate success, when the books were first released the brothers were harshly criticized. Although the stories were called children's tales, they were not considered suitable for children. As a result, many changes were made through subsequent releases. For example, the brothers removed the sexual references from stories such as "Rapunzel." In the original story, Rapunzel innocently asks why her dress is getting tight around her belly, and thus naively reveals to the witch her pregnancy and the prince's visits.[10]

The work was first translated into English in 1823, and has since been translated under numerous titles including *Grimms' Fairy Tales*. Due to their universal appeal, several stories became very well-known and inspired a myriad of print, theatrical, operatic, balletic, and cinematic

---

[9] "Grimms' Fairy Tales." Wikipedia, Wikimedia Foundation, 12 Dec. 2022, https://en.wikipedia.org/wiki/Grimms%27_Fairy_Tales.
[10] "Grimms' Fairy Tales." Wikipedia.

adaptations. The best-known stories include "Hansel and Gretel," "Snow White," "Little Red Riding Hood," "Sleeping Beauty," "Tom Thumb," "Rapunzel," "The Golden Goose," and "Rumpelstiltskin."[11] But there are many weird, quirky, and sometimes incredibly dark stories you may not have heard of.

One of these stories is "The Stolen Farthings." A farthing is the former monetary unit and coin of the United Kingdom. Minted between 1860 and 1956, the monetary value of the coin was equal to a quarter of an old penny.

As the story unfolds, a couple are having dinner with their house guest. At midnight, the guest witnesses a little girl in a white dress come into the house through the front door and go straight into the next room. Soon afterwards he sees her exit the room and walk out of the front door as quietly as she came in. The girl returns to the house the next day and the day after that. Bewildered, the guest describes what he has seen to the father. The father claims he never saw the girl.

One night, after the girl returns to the house yet again, the guest peeks into the room. He sees the little girl sitting on the floor, digging up something between the floorboards. The next day, he reports what he saw to the mother and she tells him that the apparition is likely the couple's daughter who had died a month ago.

The child was given two farthings from the mother and was planning on giving them to a poor man. However, she changed her mind and decided

---

[11] "Grimm's Fairy Tales." Encyclopædia Britannica, Encyclopædia Britannica, Inc., https://www.britannica.com/topic/Grimms-Fairy-Tales.

to hide them between the floorboards, so she could use the money to buy biscuits. Unfortunately she died before she could use the money. Following her death, her spirit came back to check on the farthings. Once the family donated the farthings to the poor man, the ghost stopped coming to the house.[12]

---

[12] "The Stolen Farthings." Wikipedia, Wikimedia Foundation, 27 Apr. 2022, https://en.wikipedia.org/wiki/The_Stolen_Farthings.

*iv. A Child's Coins (Kodomo no okane)*

# A Child's Coins (*Kodomo no okane*)

*Characters:*

**H:**  Husband
**W:**  Wife
**O:**  Mr. Okabe, neighbor across the street
**S:**  Mrs. Sensaku, next door neighbor

*During the Edo and Meiji periods, numerous Japanese towns developed and prospered around copper mines. Copper was mainly used in casting Japanese mon coins.*

*The mon was the currency of Japan from the Muromachi period in 1336 until the early Meiji period in 1870. The mon coins were used primarily by ordinary people to purchase commodities.*

*The following story is about two shiny new copper mon coins.*

|  |  |
|---|---|
|  | *A family of three are seated together around the dinner table* |
| **W:** | I hate to say it, but this house no longer holds the happiness it once did for our family. |
| **H:** | Go ahead and say it.<br>I feel the same way. |
| **W:** | Oh, why can't we leave this place?<br>Why can't we start over in another house, in another town? |
| **H:** | I never said we couldn't. |

**W:** Then let's do it.
Let's leave this place right away!
*A few days later, the family packed up their belongings and moved out without saying a word to anyone. The house that was once bright and lively now stood dark and vacant.*

**O:** (*Looking out the window*)
The family across the street sure left in a hurry.
I wonder why?
Empty houses are spooky.
Even with the sun high in the sky at noon, the place looks dark and foreboding.
It would be nice to have another family move in to that house.
It'll liven up the place once again.

*Just as Okabe was about to turn away from the window, a small child appeared outside in the distance. Small, pale, and dressed in white, she walked slowly down the street toward the vacant house. Mesmerized by the child's appearance, the neighbor stood watching out of his window.*

*The child walked up to the vacant house, opened the door and went inside.*

**O:** That's strange. That child walked into that house as if it were her own.
Why did she go inside that dark house with no one in it?
Aren't children afraid of the dark?

*About ten minutes later, the same child walked out of the house, closed the door behind her and disappeared down the same street.*

**O:** What an odd thing to happen this time of day.

I better go have a look around that house and see what kind of mischief that child was up to?

*Okabe walked over to the vacant house and went inside. It was dark and empty with only a narrow beam of light coming through the window. He squinted his eyes to see. Suddenly, a strange chill came over him. He shuddered.*

**O:** Brrrr! There's nothing here.

Everything is as they left it.

Empty except for the cupboard and the stove.

(*As he slowly turns around*)

Aaahhh!! (*Jumps with fright*)

Oh! It's just a mirror.

I almost gave myself a heart attack!

I didn't realize I looked so scary in the dark.

It doesn't make sense.

Why would a child walk into an empty house, leave it untouched, and then leave?

*Unable to find anything wrong, Okabe returned home. The next day, he happened to be passing by his window when the same child walking down the street toward the empty house caught his eye. It was noon.*

**O:** Blessed be– she's back!

I wonder if she is going to go into that house again?

Blessed be – she did!

Why?

*Okabe was frozen still in front of the window, unable to move a muscle. He watched in nervous anticipation. Just as before, after ten minutes had passed, the child came out of the house. She closed the door behind her and disappeared down the street.*

**O:** What on blazes is going on here?

I have to go see.

*Okabe rushed out of his house and ran into his former neighbor's vacant house.*

**O:** Hmmm- just like before, nothing unusual.

Ugh! There's that mirror again.

What a place to put a mirror!

A person can die of fright in this house.

So why did she return to this house?

I don't recognize her.

She can't belong to the family that once lived here.

Did they forget her?

Impossible!

*The next day, Okabe had forgotten about the child and was going about his business when she appeared once again at high noon.*

**O:** She's come back! That makes three days in a row.

Why does she keep coming here at exactly the same time every day?

This time I am going to follow her into the house!

*As before the young child entered the house alone. She was fully concentrating on the task at hand and did not notice the man who followed her into the house. She moved swiftly in the dark and walked straight into a back room. Okabe stealthily followed her, although he had difficulty seeing in the dark. The door to the room was slightly ajar and Okabe drew closer in order to gaze through the opening.*

**O:** Why, she is sitting on the floor.

What is she doing?

She seems to be poking and digging in between the floorboards.

What is she searching for?

*The child did not notice that she was being spied on and continued to frantically dig in between the floorboards, growing more anxious as the minutes ticked away. Then suddenly, she stopped, rose up and started toward the door.*

**O:** Oh no! She will see me!

I have to get out immediately.

*Okabe dashed out of the house and back into his house as fast as his legs could carry him. He watched for the child out of his window. Just like before, she walked out of the house, closed the door behind her, and disappeared down the street.*

*With the child gone, Okabe decided to go back into the house to search in between the floorboards. He had to find out what the child was looking for.*

**O:** I don't think she will be back today.

This is my chance to investigate.

*He entered the house and brought a candle with him this time. He walked to the back of the house and went into the small room where he had seen the child earlier.*

**O:** Let's see, she was sitting right about here.

And she was digging around these floorboards here.

*He placed the candle on the floor and began to pry the boards up one by one. What he saw surprised him.*

**O:** What's this? It gleams in the candle light!

Why, it's two shiny copper coins.

Two mon!

So, that's what she was after. Money!

But why? And who left two mon under the floorboards?

Perhaps this money belongs to the family that lived here.

But why would she want it?

I better talk to Mrs. Sensaku next door.

Perhaps she knows something.

What am I saying?

She is the neighborhood snoop, she knows everything!

Surely she must have seen the child coming and going like I did.

**O:** *Knock, knock, knock!*

Sen-san! Are you home?

Sen-san?

**S:** *(Opens the door)*

Oh! Okabe-san! What a surprise to see you!

**O:** What do you mean surprise?

Weren't you spying on me from your window just now?

**S:** Whatever do you mean?

**O:** Err —well I am sorry to drop by unannounced, but I had to talk to you.

**S:** Oh?

**O:** Have you seen the little girl who has been coming to the house next door for the past three days?

**S:** What little girl?

**O:** Ahh —you must have seen her! You are such a busybody; you know everything that goes on in this neighborhood!

**S:** Okabe-san!!!

**O:** You must have seen her.

Small child, dressed in white?

**S:** No, I can't say that I have seen anyone matching that description.

**O:** She came to the house next door three days in a row!

Always at noon.

I know you have been spying out of your window.

You always do.

**S:** Okabe-san! Are you accusing me....

The only person I saw going in and out of the house next door was you!

**O:** THERE WE HAVE IT!!!

**S:** W-well, you forced me to admit it!

**O:** So you know there is something strange going on next door.

**S:** The only thing strange is you Okabe-san!

**O:** Sensaku-san! You certainly are one to talk about strange…

**S:** Okabe….

**O:** Look, as I said, this child has visited the house for three days in a row.

She goes in and comes back out after ten minutes.

Today I followed her.

She went into the back room.

She was digging around the floorboards.

She obviously didn't find what she was looking for and left.

And I am certain she will be back tomorrow.

**S:** Have you had any sake Okabe-san?

**O:** I have not been drinking Sensaku-san!

I am not drunk!

I went back into the house after she left and pulled up the floorboards.

I found these!

(*He shows her the two copper coins*)

**S:** (*Her face suddenly grows pale*)

Oh! You said you found these under the floorboards in the back room?

**O:** Yes.

**S:** Can you describe the child once again please?

**O:** Well, like I said. She is small, perhaps four years of age.

She is very pale looking. She wears a white dress.

She has long dark hair….

**S:** (*Interrupts him abruptly*)

Okabe-sane! Stop!

No, it can't be.

**O:** What can't be?

**S:** Those coins.

I gave those shiny new coins to our neighbor's daughter one month ago.

**O:** Neighbor's daughter?

**S:** Yes, they had two children, a boy and a girl.

The girl was four years old.

**O:** Was four years old?

**S:** Yes, she died suddenly one month ago.

**O:** Four is an unlucky number.

Ichi, ni, san, shi….one, two, three, four…shi sounds like death!

**S:** Yes, four is an unlucky number Okabe-san.

Poor little thing, rest her soul.

The family was devastated after she passed away.

That is why they moved out of that house.

It was filled with sadness for them.

**O:** What does this have to do with the coins and the little girl who comes to the house?

**S:** I gave those coins to that little girl just before she died.

I asked her to give them to the blind beggar down the street.

Oh! She was such a precocious child!

**O:** I don't understand.

**S:** Okabe-san! For a man of your advanced years, you are very naïve!

I gave those coins to the little girl to give to the blind beggar. She instead hid them under the floorboards of her bedroom so that she could buy sweets with them later.

She died before she could use the coins.

**O:** So the child who has been coming to the house is not a child at all?

It is a g-g-g…..

**S:** Ghost! (*Lurches toward him*) Okabe-san.

**O:** Aaahhh! Don't do that!

You're scary enough without pretending to be a ghost!

My nerves are on edge to begin with.

I followed a ghost into that house!

**S:** Okabe-san! Will you get serious for a minute!

**O:** I am quite serious madam!

I am seriously afraid of ghosts.

**S:** There may be a way we can satisfy her spirit and keep her from returning to her old house.

**O:** We can? How?

**S:** If we give these coins to the blind beggar the deed will be done. Spirits who walk this earth are the souls of the departed with unfinished business.

That girl's spirit will come to the house as long as those coins remain there. But, if we give them to the blind beggar, her spirit can finally rest.

**O:** Do you really think it will work?

**S:** What do we have to lose?

**O:** Sleep! I will lose sleep if it doesn't work and I have to think about being haunted day after day by the child's ghost.

**S:** Okabe-san! Are you a man or....

*Later that day, Okabe found the blind beggar on the street corner and gave him the coins as he was instructed to do. The next day...*

**O:** Well, it's high noon. This is the time she usually comes to the house.

I sure hope this works.

(*Clasps his hands together and mumbles a prayer*)

*Soon an hour passes by and then another, and another.*
*There is no trace of the child ghost.*
*He waits until early evening and still she does not appear.*

**O:** So that was it.

Mrs. Busybody was right!

The little girl had unfinished business and could not cross over to the other world until the deed was done.

Now that I gave the coins to the blind beggar, she can finally rest in peace.

*Just then the front door opens wide.*

**O:** Aaaahhhh! SEN-SAAAAAN!!!!

*v. I Want a Divorce (Rikon shitai)*

# I Want a Divorce (*Rikon shitai*)

*Characters:*

**H:** Hachigoro

**K:** Kumagoro

*It's often said that married couples grow more alike over the years. In fact, studies have shown that people's personalities change within the first year and a half after walking down the aisle together.*

*Since married couples have to find ways to get along on a daily basis, it's not surprising that they would experience changes in their personality as they adapt to partnered life.*

*For men, life after marriage can be rather unsettling. With marriage a man begins to see himself as a father, provider, and protector—an absolute transition away from the previous carefree life he enjoyed as a single man.*

*This story is about a changed man.*

> *Hachi and Kuma are drinking together at the izakaya, a Japanese bar, after work.*

**K:** You know Hachi, we've been coming to this izakaya every day after work for the past month now.

I never realized that you were such a heavy drinker.

**H:** I'm not.

**K:** Then why don't you go home after work?

**H:** I don't want to.

**K:** Ah! Problems with the little wife, eh? (*Laughs*)

How long have you been married Hachi?

**H:** Twelve years.

**K:** Only twelve years?

Me and the Mrs. have been together for twenty-five years! Twenty-five l-o-n-g years.

**H:** I don't think Osaki and I will last twenty-five years together.

**K:** Why not?

**H:** I'm a changed man!

**K:** Well, marriage changes everybody sooner or later.

**H:** You don't understand Kuma.

**K:** What do you mean?

**H:** I'll tell you.

Before Osaki and I were married, did I ever care about how I dressed?

**K:** No, no I can't say that you did.

You always dressed like a slob!

**H:** Exactly! (*Pauses and looks confused*)

Well no. I mean, as long as my clothes were clean, that was good enough for me.

**K:** You were a clean-dressed slob!

**H:** (*Gives Kuma a dirty look*)

After we got married, Osaki picked out my clothes for me. She insisted that I wear fine-tailored clothes in the color palette the best suits my complexion.

She said I looked more handsome that way.

**K:** (*Laughs*) Women are like that.

Why can't you change back to the way you used to dress?

You're the man of the house.

**H:** Well… I actually like dressing this way now.

It makes me feel more debonair.

**K:** Oh? Well, yes. Yes you do look *debonair*.

Funny, I didn't think you knew that word.

**H:** And another thing, before we got married I didn't care what I ate. As long as the food filled my stomach, I was happy.

**K:** Yeah, you sure ate a lot of onigiri rice balls.

(*Laughs*) You would wolf them down one after the other!

You ate like your stomach was a bottomless pit!

**H:** Osaki insisted that we go out to eat at restaurants.

**K:** There is nothing wrong with eating out once in a while.

There are a number of excellent ramen shops in this town.

**H:** Osaki insisted that we go to a restaurant every weekend.

We dined on kaiseki-ryori, the traditional multi-course Japanese dinner, once a week for the past twelve years.

**K:** Ha! All those small dishes, they are like cat's dishes.

They do well to feed a cat, but they can't feed a man like you Hachi! (*Slaps his shoulder*)

You must have been hungry afterwards.

**H:** Well…I actually enjoyed the *haute cuisine* after being introduced to it. Each course they brought out was like an art form that balanced the taste, texture, appearance, and colors of food.

**K:** Huh? What are you talking about?

**H:** The chefs only use fresh seasonal ingredients and the dishes are prepared in ways that aim to enhance their flavor.

**K:** If I didn't know you better, I'd say….

**H:** (*Interrupts Kuma*) And another thing, before we got married, my idea of entertainment was going to the yose to listen to rakugo.

**K:** Now what's wrong with rakugo? I think it's very funny.

**H:** Osaki said that rakugo is for the common people.
She said the yose was not a place for a cultured lady.

**K:** Need I remind you Hachi, you're NOT a cultured lady.

**H:** Osaki introduced me to poetry readings.

**K:** Poetry! (*Gulp*) You?

**H:** *Nagamuru ya*

*Edo ni wa marena*

*Yama no Tsuki.*

Viewing a mountain moon

Rarely is it seen so clear

In dirty old Edo.

**K:** Dirty old Edo?

**H:** That one is by the poet Matsuo Basho.

**K:** Who?

**H:** I'm leaving to Mount Inaba

pine-trees on its peak

If you pine for me—

**K:** (*Interrupts*)

What? Pine for you?

|      | Hachi, you're the last person on this earth that I would yearn for. |
|------|---|
| **H:** | Don't be so nasty Kuma. |
|      | That was a waka poem by Ariwara no Yukihira. |
| **K:** | Waka-waka-wa…? |
| **H:** | Waka poetry. Poetry written in a 5-7-5-7-7 meter. |
| **K:** | Look! I'm a carpenter, Hachi. |
|      | I know the millimeter, the decimeter, the centimeter, and the kilometer. What on earth is the 5-7-5….? |
| **H:** | Spend less time listening to rakugo and you will grow wiser. |
| **K:** | Now wait just a minute! |
| **H:** | I can't stand it any longer Kuma. |
|      | I want a divorce! |
| **K:** | You want to divorce Osaki? |
|      | But you have been married to her for twelve l-o-n-g years. |
| **H:** | Yes, twelve long years and she's changed me. |
|      | She took this poor uncouth slob and molded him into a sophisticated and charming man. |
|      | I want to divorce her Kuma! |
| **K:** | But why? |
| **H:** | She doesn't deserve me; I am just too good for her. |

*vi. There's a Frog in My Rice Porridge (Okayu ni kaeru ga iru)*

## There's a Frog in My Rice Porridge (*Okayu ni kaeru ga iru*)

*Characters:*

| | |
|---|---|
| **K:** | Kumagoro |
| **O:** | Osaki, his wife |
| **S:** | Sadakichi, their son |

*It's a well-known fact that kids say the darnedest (funniest) things. Children are honest and curious, and sometimes what comes out of their little mouths can surprise, embarrass, or amuse you. Here is a collection of short and amusing anecdotes.*

*When a 6-year-old learned that his mother was expecting her third child he said, "You've got to be kidding me!!! Do you know how hard it is to raise three kids?"*

*A child at a restaurant asked, "Why do they call them waiters when we are the ones who wait?"*

*A mother told her six-year-old son, "Money doesn't buy happiness." After thinking about it for a few minutes, he retorted, "But money buys ice cream, and ice cream makes me happy."*

꧁꧂

*Child: My father's a schoolteacher.*

*Adult: That's a fine profession. Does he like it?*

*Child: He only has one thing to complain about.*

*Adult: What's that?*

*Child: The kids.*

꧁꧂

*The following is a story about a child who outsmarts an adult.*

*On a typical Saturday morning, Kumagoro's family is gathered around the breakfast table getting ready to enjoy their first meal of the day. While the parents dine on miso soup, rolled egg omelette, and steamed rice, their seven-year-old son is served okayu, or rice porridge. The boy is not fond of okayu and devises a way to get out of eating it.*

| | |
|---|---|
| **K:** | Why aren't you eating your okayu Sadakichi? Your mother went through great trouble to prepare it for you. |
| **S:** | Great trouble? What trouble is there in simmering some rice in water? |
| **O:** | Well, if you don't think it is too much trouble Sadakichi, you can prepare your own breakfast from now on. |
| **K:** | Come on boy, eat your breakfast. |
| **S:** | I can't. |
| **O:** | And why can't you? |

S: There's a frog in it.
O: What?
S: There's a frog in my okayu.
K: There is no frog in your okayu Sadakichi.
Now stop making excuses and eat your breakfast.
S: But there is a frog in my okayu dad!
K: Well, then describe it!
S: It's green, with big bulging eyes, and it has two brown stripes running down its back.
K: What? Let me take a look! Oh my goodness Osaki! There is a frog in Sadakichi's okayu!
(*Picks the frog out of the bowl of okayu and flips it on its back on to the floor.*)
O: (*Shrieks*) What? How did it get there?

*Sure enough there was a frog swimming in the okayu and now it was lying stunned on the floor. Sadakichi was able to describe it precisely. Why might you ask? Well, the boy found the frog in the garden earlier that morning and placed it in his okayu in order to get out of eating it.*

K: Sadakichi! You…you try my patience.
S: I'd rather not dad, you're not a very patient man!
K: Just for that, you're grounded young man!
You are not allowed to go outside and play for the entire day. In fact, I am just going to sit here where I have a clear view of the front door. I will see to it that you don't sneak out of this house.
S: Aw! Dad!

**K:** That's enough. Go to your room!

Think about what you did today.

*Kumagoro settles in the living room to read his newspaper and to keep an eye on the front door. However, what he believes is just punishment for his son turns out to be just another opportunity for Sadakichi to get into mischief.*

**S:** Oh boy! With dad guarding the front door and mom busy in the kitchen, I can finally go into the *kura*.

*The kura was a traditional Japanese storehouse used to safely store valuable items. For adults, it was a place to keep dusty old family heirlooms, for seven-year-old boys, it was a place to explore and go on adventures.*

**S:** Dad keeps the key on top of this *tansu* storage cabinet.

I think I can reach it. Ugh! Almost got it....ugh...there!

*With a little effort Sadakichi steals the key to the kura and sneaks out of his bedroom window without his parents noticing.*

**S:** (*Unlocks the door and enters the kura*)

Boy, it's awfully dark and dusty in here. (*Sneezes*)

I can hardly see with the little bit of light coming in through the cracks in between the wall boards.

**S:** *(Trips over a sack of grain)* Ouch! What's this?

Oh, it's just grain. Dad keeps the good stuff upstairs.

*(Finds a ladder and climbs to the loft)*

**S:** Let's see. There has to be a candle here somewhere.

Here it is. It's awfully small, dad is such a cheapskate.

(*Lights the candle and begins to explore*)

|     | Mom and dad sure have a lot of things in here. |
|---|---|

Mom and dad sure have a lot of things in here.

What's in these boxes?

Oh, a set of tea cups and some *kakejiku* hanging scrolls depicting pine trees and cranes. Boooooring!

*Sadakichi continues to explore the loft and finds that it is not as interesting as he had imagined. Then he finds several dusty old rectangular boxes tucked away in the corner.*

**S:** What are these? There is some sort of calligraphy on one of the boxes.

(*He blows some of the dust off of the box so that he can read the calligraphy*)

It says chō…chō…chōjū…ki… no, it's gi! Gi…ga…giga. Chōjū-giga! (*He opens the box*)

Oooh! It's a long scroll with pictures of animals.

(*He unrolls the scroll*) These animals are acting like humans. These rabbits and monkeys are bathing and getting ready for a ceremony.

(*Continues to unroll*) Here is a monkey thief running from the other animals who are chasing him with sticks.

Oh! He knocks over a frog. A frog….

*Engrossed in the linear monochrome drawings, Sadakichi's imagination soars. Soon he is awakened from his dream world by his father's rough voice calling his name.*

**K:** Sadakichi! Sadakichi! Where are you hiding?

I knew he was up to something when the house fell silent.

Never trust a child who is being too quiet.

He snuck out of his bedroom window and is probably playing out here somewhere.

Sadakichi! Do you hear me?

*Sadakichi extinguishes the candle and goes downstairs. The door to the kura remains slightly open and Sadakichi quietly peers through the crack.*

S: (*In a whisper*)

Oh boy! I'm in trouble now!

He found out that I snuck out of the window in my room.

K: Sadakichi! If you don't come out right now, you will be grounded for a whole week!

S: Oh boy! A whole week! What should I do?

K: *Kumagoro is so focused on finding his son that he isn't aware of the gardening fork that is on the ground in front of him. Being the clumsy man that he is, he trips over the gardening fork and stumbles right into the well. Sadakichi, after witnessing his father's fall, lets out a laugh and comes running out of the kura.*

K: Help! Help me! Somebody help me get out of this well.

S: Dad! Is that you in the well?

K: Sadakichi! There you are. You are in big trouble young man! Wait until I get out of this well.

S: But you can't get out, can you?

K: No, the walls are too slippery for me to crawl out.

S: (*Under his breath*)

If he can't get out of the well, he won't be able to punish me!

(*Yells down the well*)

|  | OK, I will help you, but first you have to prove to me that you are really my dad. |
|---|---|
| **K:** | Of course I am your dad. Who else would be in this well? |
| **S:** | You could be the *oni* devil who has come to tempt me once again. |
| **K:** | What are you talking about Sadakichi? Stop wasting time and help me out! |
| **S:** | My dad always tells me that I listen to the *oni* devil and get into mischief. Well, I am going to be a good boy from now on and not listen to you anymore. |
| **K:** | Sadakichi! I am not the *oni* devil. I am your father. |
| **S:** | So, prove it! |
| **K:** | How shall I prove it? |
| **S:** | If I help you out, can I have some manju, the steamed bun with sweet red bean paste inside? |
| **K:** | (*To himself in a low voice*) What a time to be thinking about manju! (*To Sadakichi*) Yes, yes, whatever you want! Just get me out of here! |
| **S:** | Ha!!! You are the *oni* devil! My father said we did not have any manju at home when I asked him yesterday. (*Runs into the house leaving Kumagoro in the well*) |
| **K:** | Sadakichiiiiii! |

*Hearing her husband's cries for help, Osaki runs outside. She finds Kumagoro in the well and helps him climb out. That afternoon, the family is seated around the table once again. Kumagoro is about to punish his son for disobeying him.*

**K:** You did a terrible thing today Sadakichi.
I want you to think and think hard.

**S:** I am thinking hard dad.

**K:** Oh?

**S:** Yes, I am thinking about the frog.

**K:** The frog?

**S:** Yes, the poor frog that was knocked over by the monkey. Just like you when you knocked the frog over this morning.

**K:** Monkey? Sadakichiiiiii!!!!!

# Börte's Kidnapping: A True Story

Empress Guangxian Yisheng is the posthumous name given to the woman who had simply been known as Börte, the first wife of the great Genghis Khan—the man who united the many nomadic tribes of the Mongol steppe and became their universal sovereign.

Despite her eventual rise to prominence, very little is known about Börte's early life. The limited information we have about her comes from *The Secret History of the Mongols*, the oldest surviving literary work in the Mongolian language. It tells us that she was born around 1161 to parents Dei-Sechen and Tacchotan. As the chieftain of the Olkhonud tribe Dei-Sechen strived to maintain a cordial relationship with the Borjigin, the tribe to which Börte's future husband Temüjin (Genghis Khan's birth name) belonged to. In those days Mongol politics often relied on arranged marriages to solidify alliances between the different clans and to ensure the stability of Mongolia. Accordingly, Dei-Sechen entered into an agreement with Temüjin's father, Yesügei Bagatur, betrothing the ten-year-old Börte to the nine-year-old Temüjin.

Following the engagement, Yesügei delivered Temüjin to the Olkhonud clan, where he was to live and serve Dei-Sechen. It was customary for Mongolian men to pay a "bride fee" to their future father-in-law or offer labor as an alternative.

On his way back home Yesügei encountered an encampment of Tatars celebrating a wedding feast. The Tatars had long been Mongol enemies and Yesügei was known for having killed one of their own in a battle eight years earlier. Still, he decided to join the feast. One of the Tatars recognized him and offered him poisoned food under the pretense of hospitality. Although Yesügei became quite ill he managed to escape back to his family's camp, where he died three days later.

Upon learning of his father's demise Temüjin returned home to claim his father's position as chieftain, but the tribe refused him and abandoned the family, leaving them without protection. For the next several years the family lived in complete destitution. In 1177, Temüjin was captured by his father's former allies, the Tayichiud. He was enslaved and humiliated by being shackled in a cangue (a type of portable pillory used to punish petty criminals). With the help of a sympathetic guard Temüjin managed to escape his captives under the cover of night by hiding in a river crevice.

The following year he went in search of Börte. Dei-Sechen was delighted to learn that Temüjin had returned for his daughter and commenced with the wedding. The young couple were married against a backdrop of war and tense clan rivalries in Mongolia. Börte was merely seventeen at the time. With his father-in-law's permission Temüjin took Börte and her mother to live in his family's yurt, which was situated along the Senggür River. An exquisite black sable jacket served as the young bride's dowry.

Soon after the wedding, the Merkits, a confederation of three tribes inhabiting the basin of the Selenga and Orkhon Rivers, attacked the family camp. Temüjin, his family, and friends were able to escape on their horses; Börte, unable to find a horse was left behind. She was taken captive by the Merkits and given to Chilger Bökh, a Merkit warrior and the younger brother of the Yehe Chiledu.

Temüjin's mother Hoelun, who like Börte was from the Olkhonud tribe, had been engaged to the Merkit chief Yehe Chiledu. She was abducted by Temüjin's father while she was being escorted home by her fiancé. It was evident that the raid and abduction of Börte were in retaliation for the abduction of Hoelun many years earlier.

Temüjin was deeply distressed by the abduction of his wife and vowed that he would bring her back. Eight months later with the aid of his allies Toghrul (also known as Wang Khan) and Jamukha (a Mongol military and political leader), he made good on that promise.

Upon seeing Börte once again, Temüjin was surprised to learn that she was pregnant. She later gave birth to a son they named Jochi. Since Börte had been given to a Merkit warrior as a wife during her captivity, it left doubt as to who the real father of the child was. Börte ultimately gave birth to four sons and five daughters. Temüjin claimed Jochi as his own son, but his brothers would not accept him as ruler and Temüjin was forced to choose another son to succeed him. Jochi became leader of the Golden Horde instead. At its peak the vast territory of the Golden Horde extended from Siberia to parts of Eastern Europe.

As was common among powerful Mongol men, Temüjin had many wives and concubines. He gave several of his high-ranking wives their own camps to live in and manage, but Börte remained the most influential and important person in his life, along with his mother Hoelun. He made her the head of the first Court of Genghis Khan and the Grand Empress of his Empire. Genghis Khan passed away in 1227. Börte died just three years later and was buried in what is now known as the Xinjiang Uygur Autonomous Region.

In 2019, researchers uncovered genetic evidence supporting the claim that Jochi was Genghis Khan's first true-born son.

*vii. Börte's Kidnapping (Borute no yūkai)*

# Börte's Kidnapping (*Borute no yūkai*)

*Characters:*

| | |
|---|---|
| **B:** | Börte |
| **T:** | Temüjin, her husband |
| **TB:** | Togtoa Behi, Merkit Warrior |
| **C:** | Chilger Bökh, younger brother of Merkit chieftain Yehe Chiledu |
| **BO:** | Boorchi, Temüjin's friend |

*The word "kidnapping" originated in the late seventeenth century. It was first used to describe the act of "stealing children to provide servants to the American colonies." [13] Today the word kidnap includes all abductions, of both children and adults. Whether it is done for revenge, ransom, or some other reason, each abduction creates an overwhelming absence in the lives of the people whose loved ones are taken away.*

*When the young bride Börte was kidnapped by a rival tribe in Mongolia, her husband Temüjin (the birth name of Genghis Khan) was deeply distressed and remarked that his "bed was made empty and his breast was torn apart."[14] He was determined to bring her back!*

---

[13] "Kidnap - Definition, Meaning & Synonyms." Vocabulary.com, https://www.vocabulary.com/dictionary/kidnap.
[14] de Rachewiltz, Igor. "The Secret History of the Mongols: A Mongolian Epic Chronicle of the Thirteenth Century." Western Washington University, The Australian National University, Dec. 2015, https://cedar.wwu.edu/cgi/viewcontent.cgi?article=1003&context=cedarbooks.

*Some scholars have described this event as one of the key crossroads in Temüjin's life, which moved him along the path towards becoming a conqueror.[15]*

> *In 1178, news of young Temüjin's marriage to Börte spread through the Mongol steppe like the wind. For some, it became a celebrated victory which drew them back to the clan they had once abandoned. For others, it rekindled an old flame of vengeance.*

**TB:** (*Sashaying into Chilger's yurt [16]*)

Sooooo, have you heard the news?

**C:** (*Sternly*) What are you talking about Togtoa?

**TB:** (*In an effeminate manner*)

Everybody up and down the Orkhon River is gossiping about it…..(*Pokes his finger on Chilger's chest*)

Gossip, gossip, gossip.

**C:** Stop that!

Get to the point Togtoa!

I don't have the time or the patience for your games today.

**TB:** The point? (*Laughs*)

Come, come now big chieftain's little brother, don't be so mean to Togtoa.

I am your friend and comrade in arms after all.

---

[15] History.com Editors. "Genghis Khan." History.com, A&E Television Networks, 9 Nov. 2009, https://www.history.com/topics/china/genghis-khan.

[16] A portable, round tent covered and insulated with skins or felt and traditionally used as a dwelling by several distinct nomadic groups in the steppes and mountains of Central Asia.

| | |
|---|---|
| **C:** | Cut it out already! |
| | Say what you have to say or get out! |
| **TB:** | Okay, okay big meanie! |
| | (*Whispers in Chilger's ear*) |
| | Yesügei's son has married the daughter of Dei-Sechen. |
| **C:** | He has, has he? (*Grimacing*) |
| **TB:** | Everyone says that the newlyweds are in love and so happy! |
| **C:** | Their newfound happiness won't last long. |
| | I swear to Tengri[17] in Heaven—I'll see to it! |
| **TB:** | (*Grinning a maniacal grin*) The time has come? |
| **C:** | It's a shame that we can't take our revenge on Yesügei for disgracing our great chief Yehe Chiledu. |
| | But we can punish his offspring. |
| | Make him pay for the kidnapping of Hoelun all those years ago. |
| **TB:** | Oh goody!! |

*A few short months later as the first clan members began to rejoin the house of Temüjin, 300 Merkit warriors led by Togtoa Behi descended on the Borjigin encampment.*

*It was during dawn's early hours and Temüjin and his new bride were still asleep when they were suddenly shaken from their slumber by the thundering sound of horses' hooves in the distance.*

| | |
|---|---|
| **B:** | Temüjin! What's happening? |

---

[17] The All-Encompassing God of Heaven in the traditional Turko-Mongolian religious beliefs.

T: I don't know Börte, but I am going to find out!

*(Rushes out of the yurt)*

There is a great dark cloud of dust rising in the distance.

It grows closer by the minute.

Whoever they are we have no forces to resist them.

I have to warn everyone and make sure they get away safely.

*(Returns to the yurt and turns to Börte)*

We are under attack! Find a horse and ride away as fast as you can! Save yourself! Go!

*Temüjin leaves Börte, a skillful rider and archer, on her own as he attempts to get his mother and his brothers to safety. The Merkit reach the encampment and begin terrorizing the tribe. In the confusion created by people fleeing and horses trampling the grounds, Börte is left standing alone—unable to find Temüjin, unable to find a horse, and unable to get away to safety.*

TB: Now where is Yesügei's little runt?

Teeeemi…..Temüjin, come out, come out wherever you are.

Big bad Togtoa has a surprise for you.

*(Suddenly spots Börte standing alone)*

Ah, but what do we have here?

A majestic prize just waiting to be plucked!

Won't the big chief's little brother be happy?

Ah-ha-ha-ha!

*(Sweeps Börte up on his horse and gallops away)*

B: *(Kicking and fighting)*

Nooooo! Let me go!

Stop! Stop!!!

Are you wearing women's perfume?

*Later that day, Togtoa and the other Merkit warriors return to their own encampment drunk with victory. Togtoa prances over to where Chilger is seated waiting for them. Börte's hands are tied and there is a rope around her neck. She is led by Togtoa who acts as if he is walking his pet.*

C: I trust that the mission went well?

TB: Oh! My dear Chilger!

They fled at the first site of our horses.

They didn't even fight back.

We were going to kill Temüjin, but he too fled—like a coward.

C: (*Laughs heartily*) I expected as much from that worthless, no good son of Yesügei.

And what do we have here?

TB: The spoils of war precious!

A gift for you!

(*Gives Börte a shove toward Chilger*)

Her cowardly husband fled and left her behind.

C: What a shame. (*Turns to Börte who is lying at his feet*)

Come now, let's take a look at you.

(*Holding Börte's chin up*)

Hmmm —you are even more beautiful than Hoelun.

You will make a good wife and give us many Merkit children.

**B:** (*She spits in his face*)

Never!

*As Chilger wipes Börte's saliva from his face, she squirms away.*

**TB:** Oh look! (*Laughing*)

These Olkhonud women morph into a Mongolian Death Worm when confronted!

Be careful my precious!

The worm is known to spray venom at its attacker! (*Laughing*)

**C:** Not so fast my dear! (*Stands up and goes after her*)

Where do you think you are going?

*With her legs free, Börte turns and kicks him. Chilger is caught off-guard and falls backward landing on his back. The Merkit warriors laugh heartily at the spectacle.*

**B:** Go to Hell!

**TB:** Oh my goodness! She is a true shape shifter!

Now she's become a Siberian Musk Deer – she kicked him while she was trying to get away! Ah-ha-ha-ha!

Careful precious! These deer have fangs too!

She may bite you next!

Spunky devil….(*batting his eyelashes*)

**C:** (*Gets up and grabs Börte by the shoulders and slaps her*)

You are spirited like a fine *Takhi*! I like that!

(*She headbutts him as hard as she can*)

Ooof! You wench!

(*He slaps her again*)

I'll break you like I have broken all the fine horses I have captured!

**B:** I can tell you spend all your time with horses.

You stink like one!

*In the meantime, Temüjin is highly distressed and plots how to reclaim his wife.*

**T:** We can execute a surprise raid on the Merkit camp and take Börte back by stealth!

But the wretched Merkit won't be satisfied until I am dead.

If we steal her back, they will return with a larger force and annihilate us all.

We have nowhere to escape to and no force to resist the attackers.

If we are going to retake Börte, we must also wipe out the Merkit leaving no chance for them to revive themselves.

We have to ally ourselves with someone and attack them using the abduction of Börte as a pretense.

*Following his mother's advice, Temüjin had visited Toghrul after his wedding to Börte. He presented his father's old ally with a gift of Börte's dowry—an exquisite black sable jacket. Now the idea of convincing Toghrul to move against the Merkit was beginning to take shape in Temüjin's mind.*

**T:** I will ask Toghrul to help me launch an attack on the Merkit. Believing that he is helping me, he will have no reason to hesitate. We will be unstoppable if Jamukha's forces join the raid, but he is my rival and will refuse if I ask him directly.

I will ask Toghrul to convince Jamukha to join us.

*As Temüjin had expected, Toghrul honored his request. Between Toghrul, Temüjin, and Jamukha, they managed to round up four great columns of warriors. Temüjin advanced the troops to Togta Behni's encampment under the cover of night. Along the way, they encountered a grey wolf. Mongolians are very superstitious people. They believe that encountering a wolf on the path to a battle signifies victory.*

*Just like the Merkit had done eight months earlier, Temüjin's forces attacked just before dawn. The brave and warlike Merkit tribesman struck back as Temüjin anticipated they would.*

**T:** These Merkit are putting up a relentless struggle around every yurt!
Burn the yurts down! Now!
*Temüjin shouted with all his might as he galloped his horse.*

*Temüjin's warriors fought fiercely, motivated by the feeling of revenge, and they began slaying every Merkit man, woman and child, without mercy.*

*In the meantime, Temüjin's brother Qasar found Börte along with an old nanny named Howagchen. He safely placed them in one of the yurts and watched over them as his brother continued to battle the Merkits.*

*When the fighting finally ceased, Temüjin's warriors gathered together the spoils of war and awaited his return. He returned with only one thought on his mind. To be reunited with his beloved Börte.*

**T:** (*To Boorchin*)
Where is Börte?

**BO:** She is safe. Qasar is guarding of her.

**T:** What happened to Togtoa Behi?

**BO:** (*Musingly*)
The coward ran away dressed in women's clothing. Before we arrived, he escaped wailing to a place called Bargujin Dell.

**T:** What about the 300 Merkid who attacked us?

**BO:** We found them all and drove our swords through their bodies.

**T:** (*Overwhelmed with hatred*)
Do the same to their offspring!
Now take me to Börte.
Why do you hesitate?

**BO:** There is something you must know.

**T:** Why are you standing in my way? Move!

**BO:** Temüjin (*Stutters*)
B-B- Börte…

*After overhearing her husband arguing with his friend, Börte emerged from the yurt. She was wearing a long flowing white silk gown as she walked slowly toward Temüjin. Everyone fell silent.*

*As she approached, Temüjin could see that she had changed in the eight months she had been in captivity. He could clearly see that she was expecting a child.*

*Fire burned in Temüjin's eyes and his nostrils flared with anger as he drew his sword. Boorchi fearing that he may kill Börte stepped in front of her to protect her.*

**B:** Step aside Boorchi.

Let me talk to my husband.

**BO:** But…my lady.

**B:** I said step aside!

*She slowly moved closer to Temüjin and kneeled at his feet.*

**B:** I didn't think I would ever see you again.

I didn't think you would come for me.

It is within your right to kill me.

Kill me if you want to.

I would rather die by your hand than by anyone else's.

*Moved by his wife's sincerity, Temüjin put away his sword and knelt by her side.*

**T:** I will always take back what is rightfully mine Börte.

By the will of Tengri, I will take it all!

*Thus began the many conquests of Genghis Khan.*

# Mongolian Pronunciation Guide

| | |
|---|---|
| Bargujin Dell | *Bar-goo-jin-dell* |
| Boorchi | *Bōr-chi* |
| Borjigin | *Bōr-ji-jin* |
| Börte | *Bōr-teh* |
| Chilger | *Chil-jeh* |
| Genghis Khan | *Jen-gūs-kŭn* |
| Hoelun | *Hō-lin* |
| Jamukha | *Jim-moo-kāh* |
| Merkit | *Market* |
| Olkhonud | *Ol-koo-ner* |
| Orkhon | *Or-kūn* |
| Qasar | *Kās-sār* |
| Temüjin | *Tĕm-gin* |
| Tengri | *Tĕn-grey* |
| Toghrul | *Ter-hu-rool* |
| Togtoa Behi | *Toy-to-ah-Ber-hee* |
| Yehe Chiledu | *Ee-chil-dee-yu* |
| Yesügei | *Yes-gee* |

# List of Illustrations

i. Sanyutei Encho Unknown author - 国史大図鑑編輯所編『国史大図鑑 第5巻』吉川弘文館、1933 年 10 月 25 日。National Diet Library Digital Collections: Persistent ID 1920452 (*Public domain*)..........................................5

ii. Asakichi Inn dating back to the Edo period Furuichi (*Compliments of Tatsuya Sudo*) ................................................................................................12

iii. The Substitute Dog (*Okage-inu*) Illustration 93270614 © Alina Melenteva Dreamstime.com (*Royalty free illustration*) ......................................................13

iv. A Child's Coins (*Kodomo no okane*) Illustration 191156145 / Ghost © Hafiza Samsuddin | Dreamstime.com (*Royalty free illustration*).......................30

v. I Want a Divorce (*Rikon shitai*)m Illustration 141917626/ © Kchungtw | Dreamstime.com (*Royalty free illustration*) ......................................................42

vi. There's a Frog in My Rice Porridge (*Okayu ni kaeru ga iru*) Illustration 238512554/ © Olga Shteinberg | Dreamstime.com (*Royalty free illustration*).48

vii. Börte's Kidnapping (*Borute no yūkai*) Illustration 79717234 © Denis Tsyrenzhapov | Dreamstime.com (*Royalty free illustration*) ............................61

***Front Cover Illustration:***

Illustration 176107018/ © Kchungtw | Dreamstime.com (*Royalty free illustration*)

***Back Cover Illustrations:***

Illustration 217278479/ © Olga Shteinberg | Dreamstime.com (*Royalty free illustration*)

Illustration 216178473 / Edo © Olga Shteinberg | Dreamstime.com (*Royalty free illustration*)

# Works Cited

Ackerman, Stefanie. "Rakugo: The Traditional Japanese Art of Storytelling." Japan Wonder Travel Blog, Japan Wonder Travel Blog, 7 Sept. 2022, https://blog.japanwondertravel.com/rakugo-japanese-storytelling-36260#:~:text=Modern%20rakugo%20material%20is%20usually,simply%20reproducing%20classic%20rakugo%20sketches.

de Rachewiltz, Igor. "The Secret History of the Mongols: A Mongolian Epic Chronicle of the Thirteenth Century." Western Washington University, The Australian National University, Dec. 2015, https://cedar.wwu.edu/cgi/viewcontent.cgi?article=1003&context=cedarbooks.

Eiraku, Kanariya. "Basic Rules for Performing Rakugo." Eiraku's 100 English Rakugo Scripts (Volume 1), vol. 1, 2022.

"Grimm's Fairy Tales." Encyclopædia Britannica, Encyclopædia Britannica, Inc., https://www.britannica.com/topic/Grimms-Fairy-Tales.

"Grimms' Fairy Tales." Wikipedia, Wikimedia Foundation, 12 Dec. 2022, https://en.wikipedia.org/wiki/Grimms%27_Fairy_Tales.

History.com Editors. "Genghis Khan." History.com, A&E Television Networks, 9 Nov. 2009, https://www.history.com/topics/china/genghis-khan.

桂文枝 (6代目)." Wikipedia, Wikimedia Foundation, 30 Nov. 2022, 桂文枝 (6代目) - Wikipedia.

"Kidnap - Definition, Meaning & Synonyms." Vocabulary.com, https://www.vocabulary.com/dictionary/kidnap.

Ohkubo, Kristine. Talking About Rakugo 1: The Japanese Art of Storytelling. 2nd ed., 2022.

"Rakugo." *New World Encyclopedia*, 2008, https://www.newworldencyclopedia.org/entry/Rakugo#cite_note-3.

"The Stolen Farthings." Wikipedia, Wikimedia Foundation, 27 Apr. 2022, https://en.wikipedia.org/wiki/The_Stolen_Farthings.

Yu, A. C. "Ochi (the Punch Line of a Joke) - Japanese Wiki Corpus." Ochi (the Punch Line of a Joke) - Japanese Wiki Corpus, https://www.japanese-wiki-corpus.org/culture/Ochi%20(the%20punch%20line%20of%20a%20joke).html.

Yu, A. C. "Rakugo (Japanese Traditional Comic Storytelling, or the Comic Story Itself) - Japanese Wiki Corpus." Rakugo (Japanese Traditional Comic Storytelling, or the Comic Story Itself) - Japanese Wiki Corpus, https://www.japanese-wiki-corpus.org/culture/Rakugo%20(Japanese%20Traditional%20Comic%20Storytelling,%20or%20the%20Comic%20Story%20Itself).html.

# *About the Author*

KRISTINE OHKUBO is a Los Angeles-based author and editor whose work emphasizes topics related to Japan and Japanese culture. While growing up in Chicago, she developed a deep love and appreciation for Japanese culture, people, and history. Her extensive travels in Japan have enabled her to gain insight into this fascinating country, which she shares with you through her work.

Her first book, a compilation of numerous travel blog articles about Japan, was published in 2016 (revised edition issued in 2022). In 2017, she released a historical study of the Pacific War written from the perspective of the Japanese people, both those who were living in Japan and in the United States, when the war broke out. Two years later, she supplemented her earlier releases with the story of an infamous twentieth century geisha, who was both a victim and an aggressor, struggling amidst a strict patriarchal culture and a rapidly changing social system. In 2019, she followed up her 2017 release, *The Sun Will Rise Again*, with a book titled *Sakhalin*. The work examines the far-reaching impact the island changing hands had on its inhabitants and resources and culminates with the tragic events which took place in August 1945.

Beginning in 2020, Kristine turned her attention to rakugo, Japan's 400-year-old art of storytelling. She released two books, *Talking About Rakugo 1: the Japanese Art of Storytelling* followed by *Talking About Rakugo 2: The Stories Behind the Storytellers*. Through a succession of biographical information, anecdotes, interviews, and rakugo scripts, the author explains why this traditional art form has endured for centuries.

In 2022, Kristine contributed her editing skills to yet another rakugo book—this one authored by English rakugo storyteller Kanariya Eiraku entitled *Eiraku's 100 English Rakugo Scripts (Volume 1)*. Following its release in August, she revisited a work she had first published three years earlier.

Originally released in January 2019, *Asia's Masonic Reformation: Freemasonry's Impact on the Westernization and Subsequent Modernization of Asia* examines how Freemasons have historically been the catalysts for change throughout Asia and the rest of the world. Utilizing careful research and setting aside the misinformation and various conspiracy theories that have emerged throughout the decades, the revised second edition presents the details and irrefutable historical facts demonstrating how Freemasons have notably been at the forefront of history, ushering in rapid change, modernization, and enlightenment.

An avid rakugo fan, Kristine once again shifted her attention to the art of rakugo in 2023. She compiled and released a collection of her own original English rakugo stories. Where applicable, the book also includes detailed historical information from which the author drew her inspiration for the stories.

As an author, Kristine believes that writing from other cultural perspectives encourages empathy and understanding, and at the same time it broadens our knowledge of the events that have unfolded over the years.

# The Rakugo Collection

**Talking About Rakugo 1: The Japanese Art of Storytelling** (*2$^{nd}$ Edition*)

Paperback – April 14, 2022

**Product details:**

Language : English
Paperback : 474 pages
ISBN-10 : 1088023606
ISBN-13 : 978-1088023600

**Talking About Rakugo 2: The Stories Behind the Storytellers**

Paperback – February 7, 2022

**Product details:**

Language : English
Paperback : 298 pages
ISBN-10 : 1087984599
ISBN-13 : 978-1087984599

**Eiraku's 100 English Rakugo Scripts (Volume 1)**

Paperback – August 17, 2022

**Product details:**

Language : English
Paperback : 350 pages
ISBN-10 : 1088061680
ISBN-13 : 978-1088061688

www.ingramcontent.com/pod-product-compliance
Lightning Source LLC
Chambersburg PA
CBHW051552010526
44118CB00022B/2675